A GUIDE TO MAKING DECORATED PAPERS

also by Anne Chambers
A Practical Guide to Marbling Paper

a guide to making

Decorated Papers

ANNE CHAMBERS

THAMES AND HUDSON

First published in the USA in 1989 by
Thames and Hudson Inc.
500 Fifth Avenue
New York, New York 10110

All the decorated papers illustrated, except for the examples
otherwise identified on pages 51-56, were made by
the author.

The line drawings are by Lucy Smith.

Library of Congress Catalog Card Number 89-50505

Typeset by Gloucester Typesetting Services
Printed in Hong Kong by Dah Hua Printing Press Co., Ltd.

to Georgie, Rourden and Lucinda
from their loving mother

CONTENTS

Anne Chambers's clear and helpful guide will enable anyone who is interested to produce attractive papers for many purposes, following a long-established tradition.

Decorated papers encompass a very wide field, ranging from gold- and silver-embossed sheets which can be bought at an auction today for around a hundred pounds each, through block-printed, marbled, paste, batik, air-brushed stencilled papers, down to florists' or other wrappings for everyday use. Wrapping papers of great charm can be found as far afield as Turkey, India and Nepal, while the variety of Japanese decorated papers is enormous.

From about the middle of the seventeenth century, though earlier examples are known, marbled endpapers began to appear in books, and later gold-embossed, paste and block-printed papers were used extensively for this purpose or as wrappers for doctoral dissertations, wedding and funeral orations, musical parts, etc., or as linings in boxes, drawers or cabinets.

Among the most important and covetable of decorated papers are the gold-embossed sheets curiously known here as 'Dutch gilt' or 'Dutch floral', 'Dutch' possibly being a corruption of 'Deutsch', or a reference to their importation through Holland. They were embossed by means of an engraved and heated copper plate to which pressure was applied, using an alloy of copper, tin and zinc to simulate gold. The press used was similar to an etching press. The principal makers were in Augsburg, Nuremberg and Fürth (there is one listed English maker) and they were active from around 1700 until well into the nineteenth century. Over six hundred different patterns have been recorded, many of them with the maker's name. The earlier ones are far superior in quality of design and execution. In England in the mid-eighteenth century one of their users was the children's book publisher John Newbery: 'Mr Newbery's gilt regiment' is how Robert Southey remembered them.

Paste paper, using coloured starch paste, is relatively simple to produce, and countless bookbinders' apprentices must have turned their hands to it, among their other chores. The celibate sisters of a German religious community, the Moravians, founded in 1722, with headquarters in the small east Saxon town of Herrnhut, had a large output, though precise attribution for these and many other decorated papers is wellnigh impossible.

Block-printed papers flourished particularly in the eighteenth century, though here again there are far earlier examples. For instance, a box in the Victoria and Albert Museum has a woodblock-printed lining paper in black with a repeating pattern of roses, supposedly using printers' pulls from Camden's *Britannia*, published in 1605. They were produced extensively in France, Germany and Italy, and Italian papers in particular have in common with paste papers the fact that they were printed, and often pre-brushed, with pigmented paste, not printer's ink. A very important centre was Bassano del Grappa, in the Veneto, where from the mid-seventeenth century to 1861 the firm of Remondini turned out hundreds of designs, many of them intended as wall coverings, though one assumes, because of their size, that only small areas such as chimney recesses or shelf surrounds were papered. The Remondini blocks were used in the first half of this century by the firm of Rizzi in Varese, and Italy was the source until recently of many excellent block-printed designs.

Marbling is said to have originated in Persia in the fifteenth century (unless one wishes to trace its ancestry back to the Japanese form, called *suminagashi*, said to date from the twelfth century) and was being made in western Europe at the beginning of the seventeenth century. The traditional method uses caragheen moss as a size, but oil marbling is described here because it is simpler. Many very early marbled pages can be found in the kind of autograph album, or *liber amicorum*, which royalty might have obtained in the Ottoman Empire at the end of the sixteenth century. Background marbling was used in the past to prevent any tampering with what was written on it—just like the security papers of today. The marbling of the edges of account books, for instance, would make the removal of any leaves easily seen.

Batik papers, despite their name which associates them with the East, were manufactured partly mechanically by a firm near Berlin, and can be found on quarter bindings of trade books in the thirties.

Also very popular in Germany at that time were air-brushed papers using stencils to achieve quite spectacular results very redolent of that particular period.

Japanese decorated papers are in a category all of their own. Some are embellished while still in the mould by bonding different sheets together, by adding bark or leaves, or by directing jets of water through a metal stencil to produce a lacy effect. Others are block-printed or coloured through stencils using a resist process. *Orizomegami* is described here because it can be produced in your kitchen without interfering unduly with its normal use, as can all the papers Anne Chambers describes. Whether you use them as endpapers in bookbinding, as linings for boxes or folders, to give an original touch to notepaper, or to wrap your Christmas or birthday presents, making them may encourage you to study them in public collections, and to look out for old or modern examples, used as endpapers or wrappers, in libraries or second-hand bookshops.

The public collections in England are the Olga Hirsch collection in the British Library, and that in the Department of Prints and Drawings at the Victoria and Albert Museum.

(In the United States there are collections at the Houghton Library at Harvard University; the Metropolitan Museum of Art, the Cooper-Hewitt Museum and the New York Public Library in New York; and in the Humanities Research Center of the University of Texas at Austin.)

Tanya Schmoller

BASIC PRINCIPLES

In the foreword, Tanya Schmoller has described the history and usage of decorated papers. This manual will show how to copy many of these old papers, without having recourse to expensive materials or specialist equipment. No processes, other than hand-blocking, are involved, and no heat processes, other than melting wax, are used. All the paints and papers are inexpensive and readily accessible, and no more work space is needed than can be provided by the average kitchen table or worktop. Apart from reproducing old papers in the original fashion, use can be made of contemporary materials, and very bold and interesting effects can be achieved. These papers, when made, have many purposes—as book-papers, decorative cards, linings for cupboards or boxes, even as wallpapers; the list is endless, so is the challenge. The results can range from simple to sophisticated, classic to contemporary, and there is a great sense of achievement as one progresses in competence and experience.

These various processes stretch the imagination, and open one's eyes to new possibilities. I find it difficult now to look at a pleasing piece of decorated paper without wondering how it was done, and trying to remember it, so that I may try to copy it. I am not deterred if the paper is old, because I feel if it could be done two or three hundred or so years ago, there is no reason why I should not be able to do it now, with patience. Equally, a modern piece of Christmas or birthday wrapping paper sometimes engages me, and I keep a piece to see how I might copy it without mechanical means of reproduction.

Because my copy will be hand-made, it will be much more irregular, and for this reason it will be more personal, something that I have done myself. The papers can then also be put to creative use: a student last year made a tiny little carrier bag of her own decorated paper, with ribbon handles, filled with chocolates: and last Christmas I was delighted to get a Christmas card from another student, who had folded a sheet of writing paper to form a card, pasted an oblong of her decorated paper to the front, and outlined it in ink. It was a most effective, and completely unique, Christmas card.

This book has been divided into sections, covering the various forms of decorated papers. Paste-grain comes first, and is the biggest section, because this is the one which is immediately successful; although it is quite easy to do, there is a vast variety of papers which can be made by this method. It is also one of the simplest in materials and equipment, since all that is needed is a paste made from flour and water, a tube or two of water-colour or some poster paint, and virtually any kind of paper that comes to hand. For the vinegar-paste, in the next section, you will need vinegar and sugar in small quantities, tubes of water-colour or poster paint, and some paper. These two most simple processes, paste-grain and vinegar-paste, can furnish the most amazing amount of completely different papers. I always enjoy doing them, either alone, or with friends or children.

Next in simplicity comes block-printing. This initially also needs no more, apart from tubes of water-colour and paper, than objects found in the kitchen—potatoes, corks, etc. For more sophisticated or experimental work, printer's inks, lino-cuts and india rubbers can be used, but, again, none of these are expensive. However, the process is quite time-consuming, especially if the design is a small one, and care must be taken if the results are to look clean and professional.

Orizomegami requires rice paper from an art shop, and some bottles of vegetable colouring from a grocer—all quite cheap. The process itself is simple and can be mastered immediately, but it takes experience to achieve really good effects. It is a well-known Japanese art form.

For stencilling, either one can make one's own stencils, or buy them from an art shop. It is easier to use felt pens than paint, and there are also excellent gold and silver pens, a little more expensive, but giving very good effects.

Craquelure/resist batik needs a block of paraffin wax from a chemist, and wire and wax crayons.

Oil marbling is done with cellulose wallpaper paste, tubes of students' oil paints, and turpentine.

However, these last three processes—stencilling, craquelure, and oil marbling—all require considerable patience to acquire a certain degree of expertise. On the other hand, paste-grain, vinegar-paste, block-printing and orizomegami can really be started by anyone over, say, the age of four or five, with very pleasing, self-congratulatory results.

I have included a section showing the work of three successful contemporary decorators of paper, all self-taught in this field, together with a description of the methods they use.

I, too, taught myself the various techniques, and have had enormous pleasure in decorating papers over the years. You need no artistic qualification or expertise—anyone can do it. The results are delightful, individual and highly satisfying.

paste-grain papers

This is the longest section in the book because, as I explained in the introduction, this technique has the most possibilities for beginners and specialists alike, and yet is one of the easiest to do, and needs few materials. This method of decorating paper was certainly used in the sixteenth century, and was called 'prints in paste' because the coloured paste was applied to a block and then printed off by hand; several methods of making designs without the use of a block were used in the seventeenth and eighteenth centuries throughout Europe, particularly in Germany, and these various methods of combing, sponging on and sponging off, blocking and splattering, are described below. But, apart from this rather gentle early work, it is perfectly possible to make very bold and strong contemporary papers by the imaginative use of tools and colours with which to treat the paste. I use the word 'tools' because I cannot think of any other which would be apt. In fact it embraces anything from a bit of cardboard, a kitchen fork, a pastry wheel, a coarse plastic hair comb, to an old soft nailbrush.

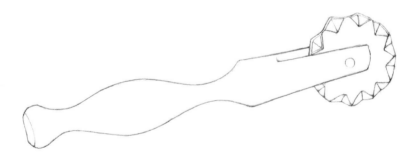

There are four sorts of paste which can be used for this technique. The perfectionist, or more experienced person, may sometimes use the rice-flour paste; it is eight times as expensive as the flour paste, but is the finest, smoothest paste for the most delicate effects. This is the one that Edwina Ellis has used for her intricate work which is reproduced on pages 55–6. The beginner will find wallpaper paste, or a made-up flour paste, perfectly satisfactory, and indeed I use this most of the time myself. As in cooking, cornflour will give a slightly smoother texture than ordinary flour.

Pastes

Cold-water wallpaper paste
Mix according to the instructions on the packet, but use less water, so that it is quite thick: the proportion will probably be 1 pt ($\frac{1}{2}$ l) of water to 2 oz (50 g) paste powder.

Flour paste
Add six parts of cold water to one part of plain flour, stirring to form a smooth paste. Bring to the boil in a saucepan, stirring continuously to avoid lumps.

Cornflour paste
2 oz (50 g) of cornflour (cornstarch) mixed with 2 fl oz (50 ml) water in a saucepan. Add $\frac{1}{4}$ pint (150 ml) of boiling water, and boil for two or three minutes, stirring continuously.

Rice paste
Rice flour makes a particularly fine smooth paste. It is very expensive, but is nevertheless well worth using for a special paper, and is mixed in exactly the same way as cornflour paste.

Materials

Paints
All paints used in this process are water-based, not oil. They can be inexpensive poster paints, powder paints, tubes of water-colour, or, more expensive but my favourite, designers' gouache. This last is in fact quite economical, because a very small amount of paint effectively colours the paste, and a few tubes of primary colours will allow you to mix your own shades.

Papers
Typing paper (bond, not flimsy), or writing paper: brown (Kraft) paper: cartridge or Ingres (from art shops), or sugar paper (also from art shops, and very cheap). Good quality lining paper from do-it-yourself shops is particularly good for children.

Brushes
Small brushes for mixing colour into paste, and one or two large 2"–4" (5 cm–10 cm) paintbrushes (from D.I.Y. shops).

Equipment
You will need a small metal whisk to beat the colour into the paste, and, if it is still lumpy, a sieve.

Bits of stiff card to cut into 'combs', and
one or two natural sponges (from chemists' shops).
Plenty of clean uncrumpled newspaper, and a damp
cloth for keeping one's hands clean.
Bowls or soup plates for holding the coloured paste.

Method Spread clean newspaper over the work area. Cut a pile of uncrumpled newspaper larger all round by several inches than the paper which you are going to decorate. This is important, because as you brush the paste over the paper, you will inevitably get paste on the surrounding area, but, by this means, you can remove the finished paper and the cut newspaper from the pile at the same time, and start clean each time. This may sound fussy, but it is very sad when a paper with which you are quite pleased proves unusable because it has got stuck to the previous piece of old pasted newspaper. It is also very important that your pile of cut newspaper is perfectly smooth, with no hidden creases or ridges in the pile. Otherwise, when you brush your coloured paste onto the paper, the ridge will show up from underneath, and no amount of brushing will get it out.

Now put some of your made-up paste into one, or two bowls. These should be wide and flat, to accommodate your paintbrush, which is quite big. Because the paints are water-soluble (i.e. completely washable) you can use cereal bowls or soup plates, which are ideal for the purpose. Then add a little colour to the paste and mix it in well, using a metal whisk. Do not worry if the colour seems a little pale, as it will dry darker. If the paste seems to have gone lumpy, you will have to sieve it through into another bowl. You cannot work with lumpy paste.

I find sometimes if I am using cold-water wallpaper paste, or flour paste, that the paste seems rather stodgy, even after the paint and a little extra water have been added; it does not spread as evenly as I would like. When this happens, it seems to help to add a drop of liquid detergent (washing-up liquid) which makes the paste smoother and more fluid. It is quite interesting to mix up two small bowls of paste-paint and add detergent to one bowl, but not to the other, and compare the results. I find the paste without detergent better for rather coarse designs, such as sponging off, while the mixture with detergent lends itself to finer designs, such as drawing a pattern with a matchstick on the paper.

Lay your paper on the smooth pile of cut newspaper, and spread the paste on it evenly and firmly with the paintbrush, going over the paper lengthways and breadthways with long, quick strokes. Do not allow the paste to dry or become hard before using one of the following techniques to decorate it.

Combed   Here a piece of stiff card, cut into teeth on one edge, or a coarse plastic comb, is used. The paper is combed overall, and can also be cross-combed to make a contemporary paper. In combing, ridges are formed where the paste is displaced; these later dry flat, but are deeper in colour, and show up as dark lines, almost three-dimensional. Although initial efforts may appear rather primitive and simple, it is possible to achieve rather beautiful papers, especially if the paper is combed, for example, in diagonal sections with a fork, or similar fine comb, to achieve a trellis effect. A plate on page 27 shows

a copy of an eighteenth-century farm account-book cover; the paste has been combed into a trellis, and little flowers made in the trellis with a wooden stick.

Splattered   A slightly more liquid colour paste is used for these papers, which were very popular as book papers in the early nineteenth century. Although they were often monochrome, sometimes several colours were prepared and used in turn. The paste is applied by splattering it with a small stiff brush (toothbrush, nailbrush, shoe-brush) through a fairly fine wire mesh held over the paper. The whole area of the paper should be splattered and the original background will show through the tiny spots, giving a pointillist impression. It is more difficult and time-consuming than might at first appear; there is also a hazard that when the paper is nearly finished, a large blob of paste-paint falls on the paper, ruining it. To avoid this, consider that you are not actually squeezing the paste-paint through the mesh, as though making a puree, but rather scraping the brush against the surface of the mesh, which you hold sideways over the paper, so that the paint is splattered off the brush. Because of this, you can work with a much drier brush than you may at first have envisaged. Indeed, to be on the safe side,

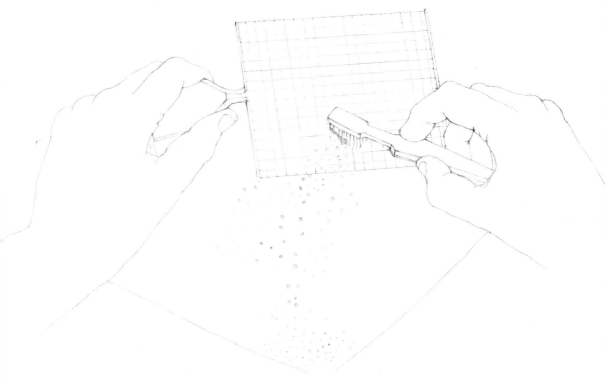

I always splatter my brush-load first of all on a piece of adjacent newspaper, so that the brush has no liquid paint on it. In this way I can also avoid getting blobs of paint on the mesh.

Sponged Off This method was used to cover many of the early account books and simple pamphlets both here in Europe and in America, the colours being nearly always rose-red or blue. The paste is brushed over the paper, as for combing, and then a clean damp sponge is gently dabbed over the paper, picking up the paste and creating a fine stipple pattern. The sponge can be small ($1\frac{1}{2}''$/4 cm) or quite big ($5''$/13 cm), and each creates a slightly different effect. An alternative which is very effective is to use a screw of newspaper and 'peck off' the paste very rapidly. This gives a much sharper effect, but you should have several little screws of newspaper to hand, discarding each as it becomes saturated and loses its sharp outline.

Sponged On A coarser type of this paper, often used in the eighteenth century in Spain and Italy, was made without first using a brush, but by dabbing the sponge into the bowl of colour, and daubing it all over the paper. Sometimes several colours were used, reds and yellows, and these papers became popular in the United States.

Pulled Paste Another eighteenth-century favourite was pulled-paste paper, which I think in fact has a curiously contemporary and surrealist look. This time two papers of similar size are laid side by side, and both brushed over with the paste-paint. They are then laid carefully face to face, and the top paper is gently rubbed over with your hand or a cloth, and then the papers are slowly pulled apart, leaving a feathery design on both papers. (This is particularly useful if you need two identical papers.) Two colours can be used, but the second colour to be brushed on should be thinner than the first. Another variation was to put pieces of soft string or felt between the sheets before pressing them together, so that when they were removed a white pattern was left. Another way was to put the pasted paper down on a smooth, cleanable surface, and then slowly peel it off.

It is more difficult than one would imagine to make these papers successfully, as they are often quite blobby if the paint has been too thickly applied.

Paste-paint can also be used in block-printing, instead of the inks or paint described in Section 3, but I did not find this very effective myself, as the consistency of the paste-paint gives a blurred outline which is rather thick and clumsy.

Block Off This is one of the methods I most enjoy using, as it lends itself to enormous and varied improvisation, and you never know what you will end up with. The paste-paint is brushed on evenly, and then various objects are impressed on the surface, to displace the paste. A piece of cork, or a thumbprint, repeated firmly at regular or irregular intervals, all make interesting patterns, especially as the displaced paste dries darker than the background, and although the ridges flatten as they dry, they still leave a deep impression.

A fine object, such as a thin fork or a matchstick, can be drawn through the paste-paint, to divide the paper into sections—circles, squares or diagonals—and then an impression can be made within the sections, giving a more formal paper.

It is important to work quickly, so that the paste does not dry. The possibilities of materials and objects with which to make the impressions are really endless. One of my favourite tools is a little wooden pastry wheel, which makes a very pretty, delicate trellis pattern with a classical appearance. When I want to make a bolder, more modern paper, I use a matchstick to divide the paper into triangles, or free-hand circles, before blocking off the sections with a strong, coarse object such as a bottle-top.

vinegar-paste papers

This has its own separate section because, although in many ways the treatments can be like those of paste-grain, the texture of these vinegar-paste papers is completely different, and never ceases to amaze me. The first reference to this process I came across, years ago, said it had been widely used by early settlers in America to decorate the walls of their houses, and when you have made some of these papers you will see why. It is at times almost like Lincrusta. I have now learnt never to colour the vinegar paste with sepia or chrome colours, because the finished paper then looks extremely like an odd form of sandpaper.

Materials *Vinegar Paste* Put 2 parts sugar (granulated or caster) to one part malt vinegar in a screw-top jar and shake vigorously together.

Paints As in paste-grain, any water-based paint is suitable—tubes of water-colour, poster paint, powder paints or designer's gouache.

Brushes A small brush for mixing up your water-colour and stirring it into vinegar paste. One or two 2″–4″ (5 cm–10 cm) paintbrushes.

Equipment Small metal whisk for mixing paint and vinegar paste. Bits of card cut into combs; corks; little lumps of Plasticine. Clean, uncrumpled newspaper.

Method As with paste-grain papers, spread the work surface with newspapers, and put the paper to be decorated on a pile of uncrumpled newspaper, cut to a size slightly larger than the paper to be used.

Put a small amount of colour into a bowl wide enough to accommodate your paintbrushes. Add the vinegar mix, stirring vigorously.

Brush the vinegar paste firmly but smoothly over the paper, lengthways and then crossways. Then the paper must be left for ten or fifteen minutes because, unlike paste-grain, the vinegar paste has to set and dry off slightly before it is able to retain an impression.

Test a corner of the paper, and if it holds an impression, then you can start to decorate it in the way you choose. It can be combed, raked with a small stick, blocked off with a piece of cork, or pecked at with a lump of Plasticine. It is not, however, so satisfactory to sponge off.

The paper will take up to three days to dry off completely, so it should be left somewhere flat meanwhile.

I did not notice any difference between caster sugar and granulated, although I had thought the surface might be coarser if the latter was used. I also emulsified one lot in a liquidiser, but, to my surprise, found the paper dried in exactly the same way as the others.

COLOUR PLATES

paste-grain papers

Opposite COMBED
Top COMBED
Bottom COMBED *rolled with incised rubber roller*

Top COMBED *copy of 18th century German accounts book*
Bottom COMBED

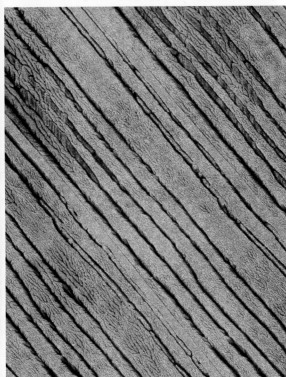

Opposite SPLATTER
Below and bottom SPONGE OFF   *Below and bottom* SPONGE ON

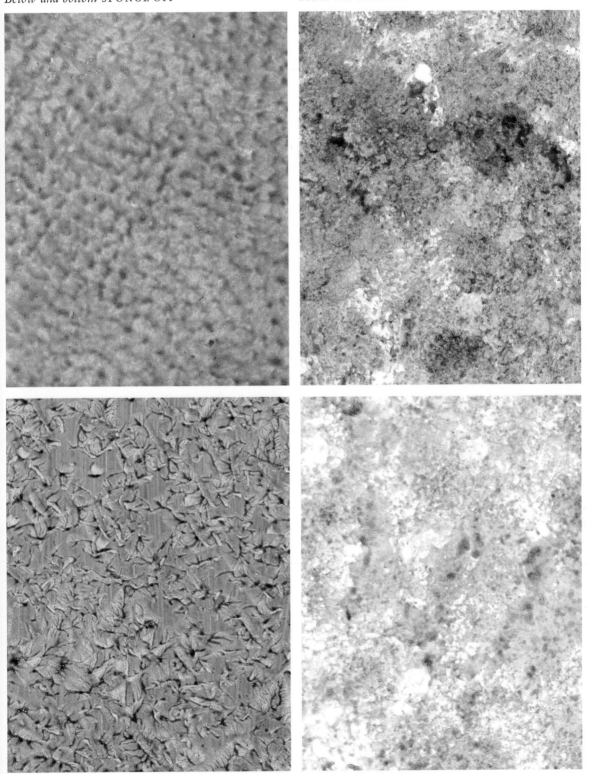

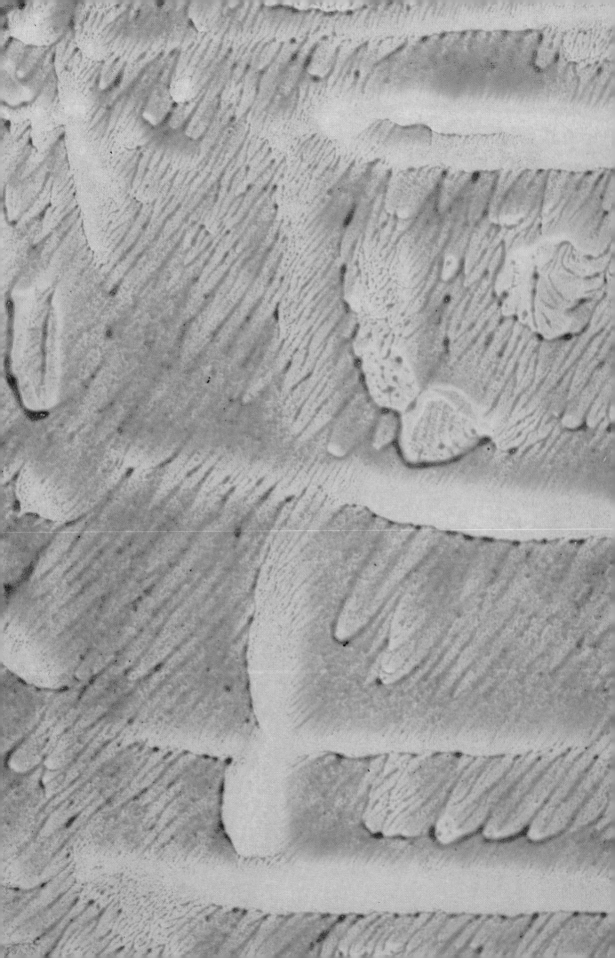

Opposite PULLED PASTE
Top BLOCK OFF *daubed with cork*

Below left BLOCK OFF *pastry wheel*
Below right BLOCK OFF *nail brush*

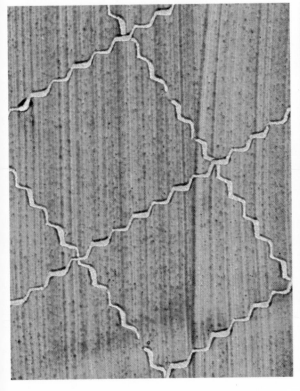

vinegar–paste papers

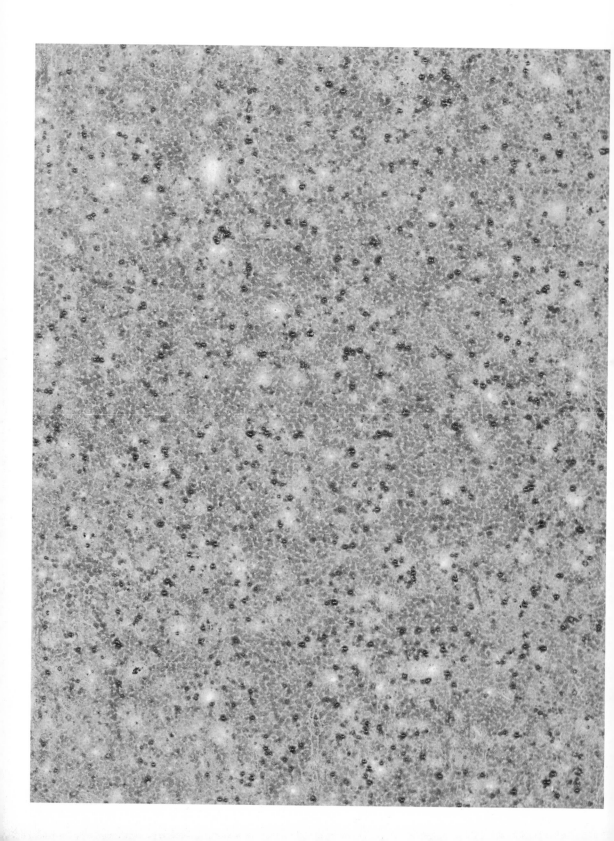

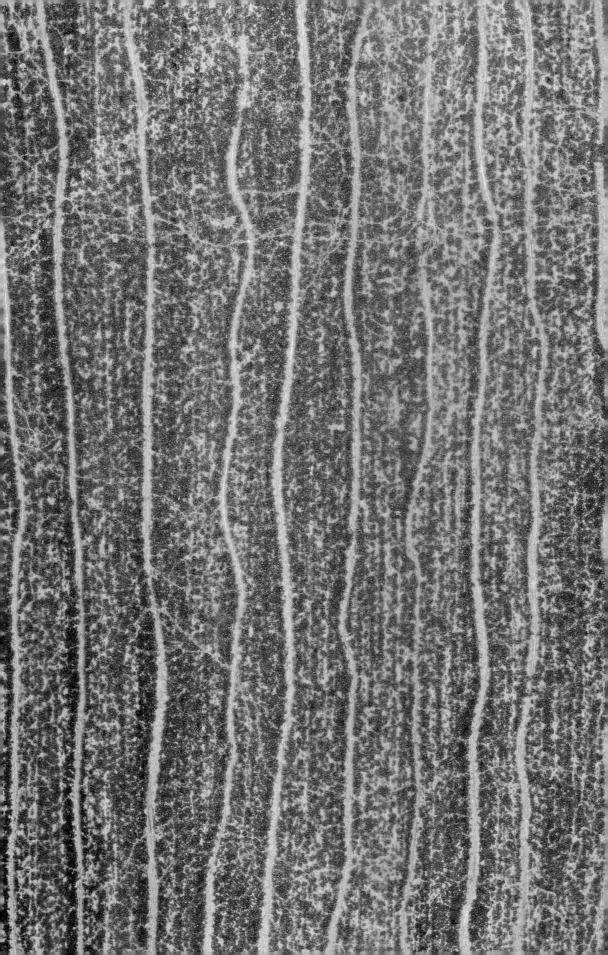

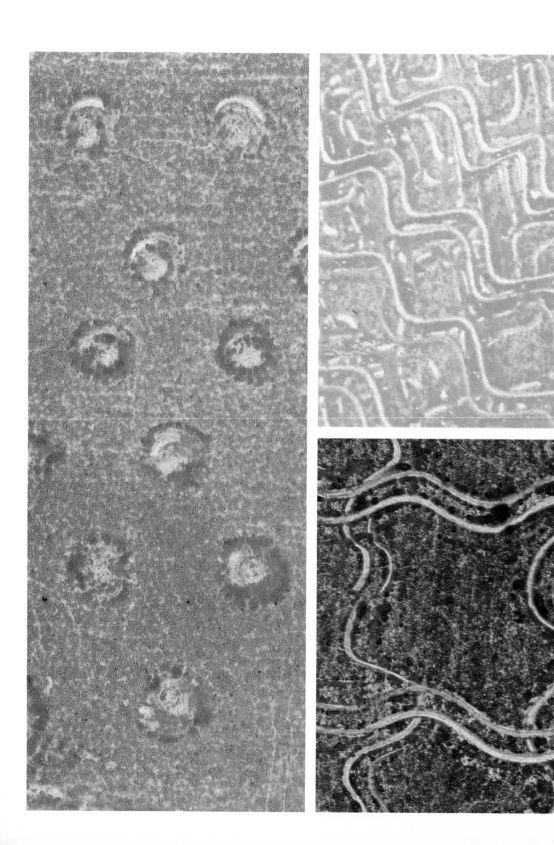

block-printed papers

BLOCK ON *pastry wheel and lino cut*

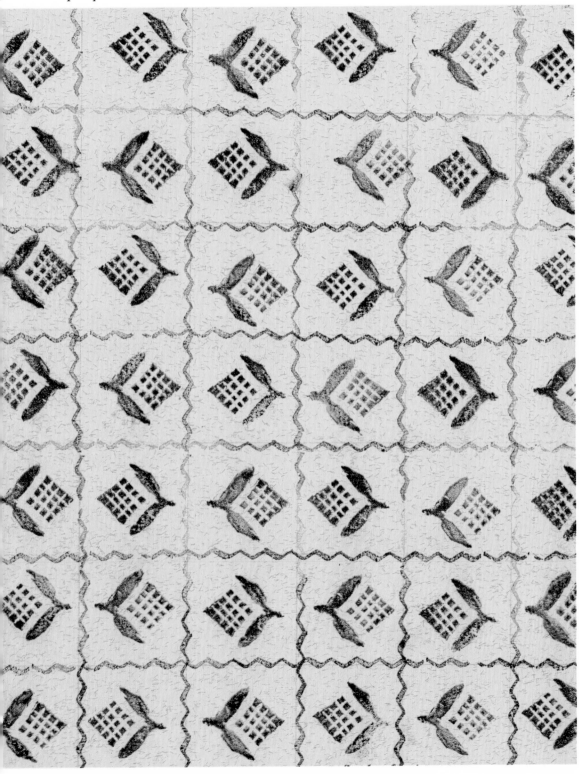

Top left BLOCK ON *lino cut*
Bottom left BLOCK ON *rubber roller*
Top right BLOCK ON *nails*

Bottom right BLOCK ON *water colour on gell based container*
Opposite BLOCK ON

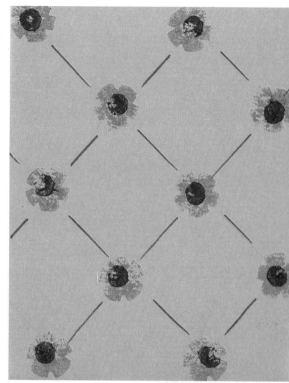

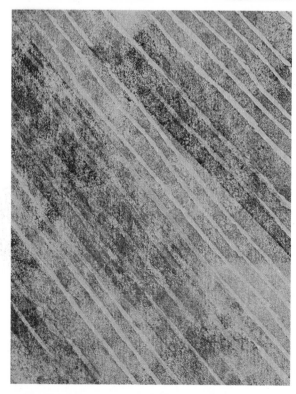

orizomegami

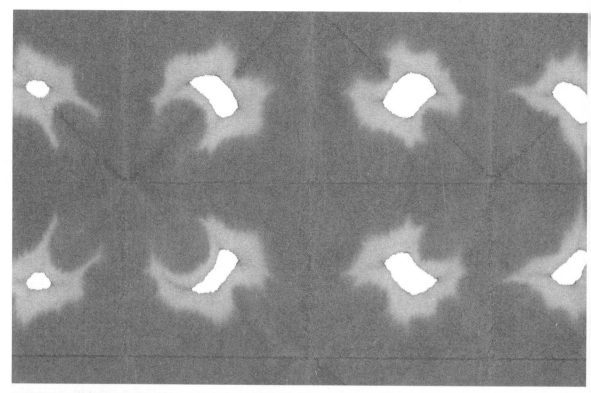

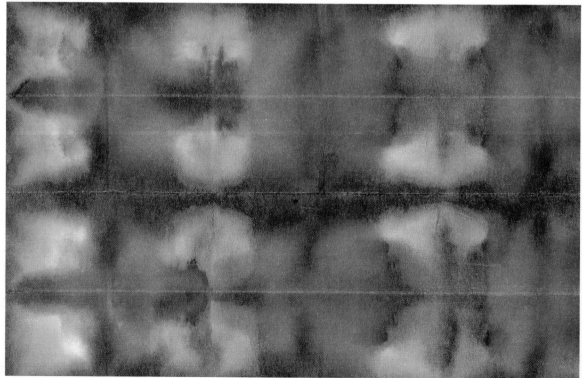

craquelure/resist batik

candle-end

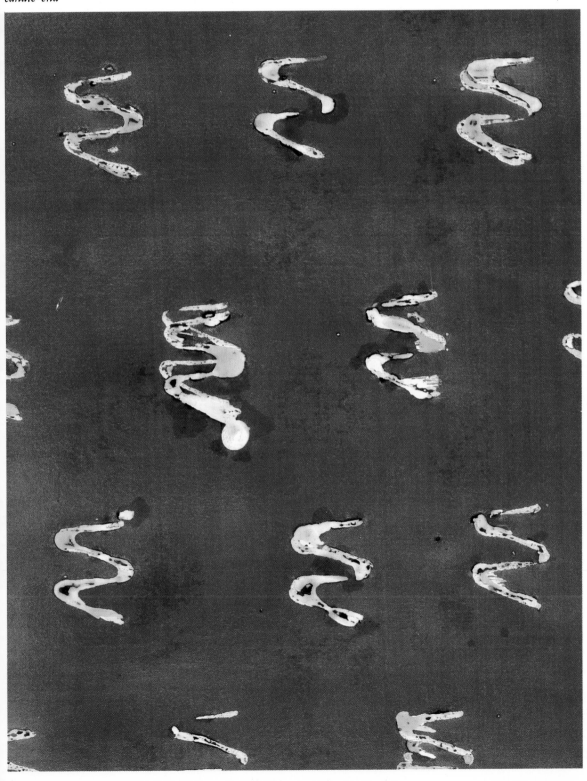

Swiss oil crayon

candle-end

stencil papers

oil marbling

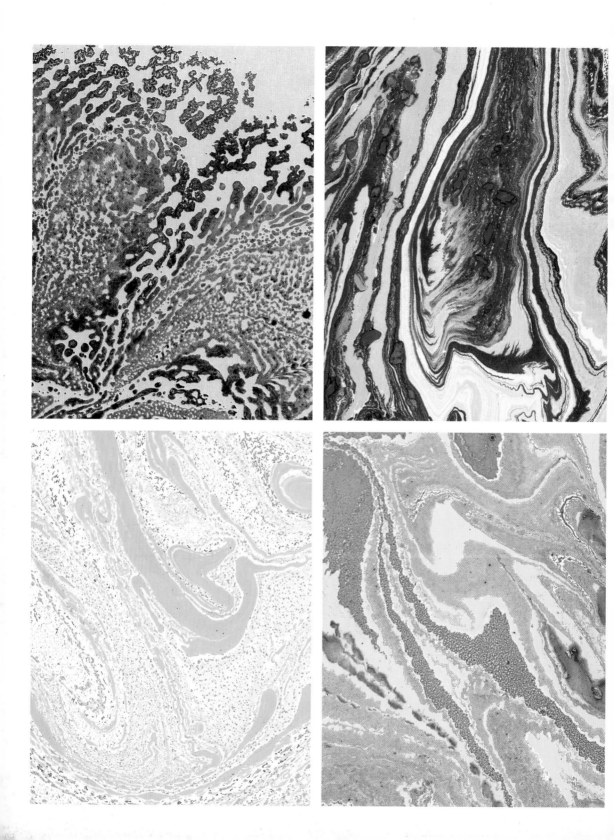

suminagashi

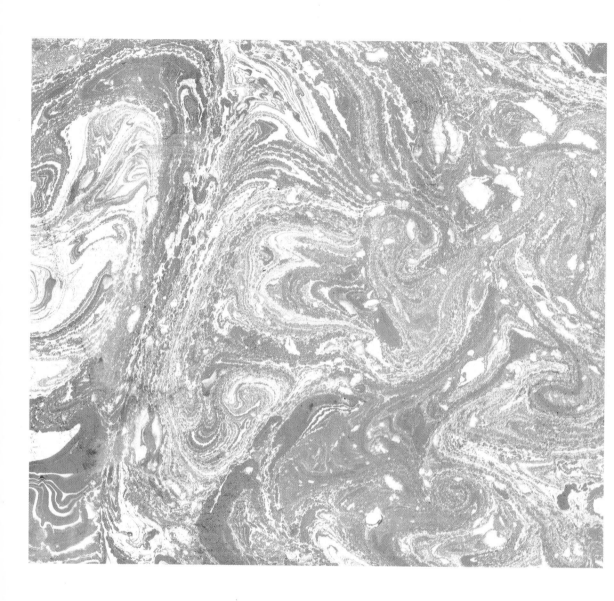

THREE MAKERS OF DECORATED PAPERS

Marthe Armitage

I was at the Chelsea School of Art in the heady days just after the Second World War. It was in the top floor of the Chelsea Polytechnic and the bomb-damaged roof was patched with tarpaulin. Lithography, illustration, lettering and fabric printing were all being taught in one long room and while I intended to become a painter, it was impossible not to be aware of other skills and their basic principles. Later, when married with children, no money and bare walls, block-printed wallpaper seemed the obvious development.

I soon became deeply interested in the making of repeat patterns and I love the slight irregularities of the hand printing and the quality of line that linocut gives; the way a pattern, confined to the rectangle of the block, comes alive when printed in repeat and hung on the wall. The first blocks were stamped out on the floor, then I came by an old offset proofing press, a piece of machinery indispensable and exasperating, allowing me certain concessions within its limited capabilities.

Carmencho Arregui

I was born in Madrid into a Basque family. My father was an artist and did not send me to school, so I had a very pleasant childhood. I was able to draw and paint all day long, trying all kinds of techniques.

In New York, where I spent one year, I learned woodcut. In Paris, I was trained by Arno Stern to run an *Atelier* of creative education, and for nine years had an *Atelier* of my own. Later, in Milan, I met Pia Isenburg, who offered me her knowledge as a bookbinder and marbler. The papers available for binding did not always suit me, so I began to paint my own.

My first approach was with potatoes, but the result was childish and the stamps too small. Then I thought of pumpkin stamps. Carving is easy and the blocks are big. I use this kind of stamp with vinyl colours (Flashe). After a while, the stamp becomes useless, which makes each pattern unique. I lay the colours directly on the stamp with a soft brush.

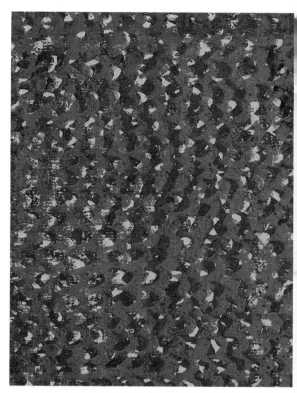

I also print with rubber rollers (the kind used for printing) which I carve with woodcutting knives. It is not like carving a flat surface; you hold your roller firmly with one hand while the other cuts the rubber. Sometimes the roller slips and you must be very quick not to cut your fingers. Once you have carved your roller, you lay typographic ink on a flat surface (like formica) and ink the roller. It is better to work on a low table so that your body weight helps the printing. Roll upwards and start on the left side of the paper to see the end of the pattern and make it match the following stripe

The patterns are, of course, very elementary and I use different systems to get a more complex result.
—When the paper is printed I pass the roller over again with a different colour for a chromatic effect.
—I put stencils between the paper and the roller.
—I move my hand horizontally, while rolling up, to create wavy effects.
—I combine two rollers whose patterns match.
—I pass the roller upwards, then from right to left.
—Before printing, I paint a background in one or more colours, using light china ink and a thick brush.

Top ROLLER AND STENCIL
Bottom PUMPKIN STAMP

Top PUMPKIN STAMP
Bottom PUMPKIN STAMP

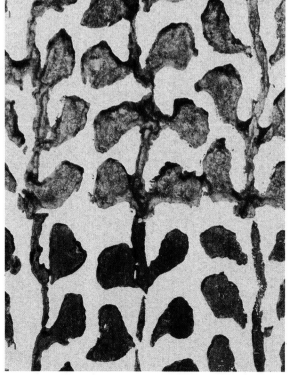

Edwina Ellis

Here are some sample paste papers using my little wood blocks along with a nail, an end of a cut-off knitting needle and a comb with most of its teeth pulled out.

I fear I have not got the consistency of the paste right and that it was a little foolish to use such thick paper as Arches watercolour paper.

They were originally for a very small book printed for me by the Libanus Press for which I produced squares of (Heritage laid) paper only about 12″ square. This accounts for the scale and busy-ness of the papers as one would get blisters doing an imperial sheet with one of the stamps.

Materials used

2 flower stamps
1 bird stamp
Two little wood squares with a design chiselled from endgrain. N.B. They would be more comfortable to use if they had a rubber-stamp handle.

I think the negative shape gives more interesting patterns.

white fat lines
A nail head: it's nice soft steel.

little flower

A knitting needle broken and filed flat, then grooves cut. I rounded the end a bit which makes it satisfying to use.

was an untampered cut knitting needle (or a pencil).

The first thing I did was a *grid* with combs or the nail, i.e. ⌐▔▔▔▔▔⌐ I picked the teeth out of a nasty pocket one. I judged by eye for putting a second row of stripes next to 1st, *or* put the comb in the last row again. (I did have fun!)

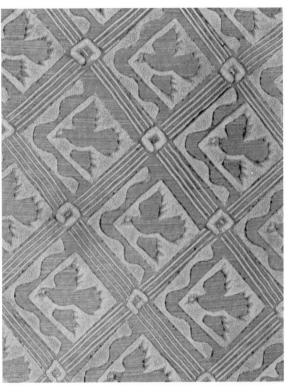

block-printed papers

This is a form of printing: the motif is dipped in or brushed with inks or paint, and then pressed down on to the paper. As I said, paste-paint may be used, but it gives a coarser effect. The pattern is repeated, and a block-printed paper is created. It is simplicity itself, but, like so many simple things, it must be done with care if a good effect is to be achieved, and of course it is fairly time-consuming, particularly with a small, closely-printed motif. However, it is possible to make very fresh and pretty papers, or very strong and original ones, with this method, and it has a depth and slight irregularity which can never be achieved with machine-made papers. The very popular Curwen Press papers were made in this way, and then reproduced, and are still available today.

Materials	*Paints or inks*	Almost any kind of paints can be used, oil- or water-based. Printer's ink of course works very well, and this can be bought quite cheaply in tubes in a good variety of colours. Acrylic paints also give a good, clear impression. There are some very good, slightly more expensive, metallic paints in three varieties of gold, which can be bought from art shops, and this can be very impressive.
	Paste	As in Section 1, paste-grain.
	Paper	Lining paper, Kraft (brown paper) cartridge, good quality typing paper, or, more expensive but giving very good results, Ingres paper (from art shops) in soft colours, particularly suitable for monochrome or gold printing.
	Equipment	It is useful to have a rubber roller for applying paint to the larger blocks, and a small sheet of glass on which to mix the paint.
		Lino-cut tools (these are quite cheap, as one wooden

handle accommodates several different cutting heads), and some artist's lino are also useful.

Apart from this, a piece of foam rubber or felt on an old plate or saucer can act as an inking pad, and most of the 'blocks' are improvised. Commercial ink pads, used for rubber stamps, can be found at stationers' shops in quite good colours.

Method   POTATO CUTS

This is the simplest way of block-printing, and one that children particularly enjoy. Cut a potato in half, and then cut a shape on the flat surface. An uncluttered shape, such as a triangle, circle or square, simple bird or flower, is best, since it is impossible to get much detail

from a potato cut. Mix up some water-based paint (do not use oil-based for potato cuts, as the potato is too watery to take it clearly): poster paint, not too thin, is excellent. Put this on your piece of felt or foam, and roll or work it well into the pad so that the paint is evenly dispersed. Then put the paper to be blocked on a little pile of un-crumpled newspaper or soft card, press the potato cut down on the ink pad, and then press it firmly down on the paper. Two simple motifs, square and circle, bird and flower, used alternately in two different colours, can make a very pleasing pattern. If the potato cut is to be kept for a short time it should be wrapped in tinfoil to keep it from going brown and shrivelled.

Carmencho Arregui (whose work and technique is shown and described on pages 52–4) found potatoes too small for her purpose, and now uses blocks cut from a pumpkin, which she discards as they become paint-sodden or blurred in outline.

OBJETS TROUVÉS

Practically any small object with a flat surface can be used as a stamp or block. A cork, either as it is, or with part of the centre cut out with a knife or apple corer, is very good. The base or rim of a small tumbler can make interlocking circles. The list of possibilities is endless. One of my best patterns was made by hammering a large-headed nail into a small block of wood, and cutting into it with a small file, to form the nail-head into a daisy shape. Another smaller nail on the opposite end of the block, inked with a different colour, formed the centre of the flower. My ubiquitous wooden pastry wheel is particularly good for forming a trellis pattern in which to put a small motif. Corrugated paper, torn into small pieces, can be inked and applied haphazardly, creating an interesting and irregular pattern.

INDIA-RUBBER CUTS

This is a more sophisticated form of blocking than the potato cut, because more exact shapes can be cut, using either a sharp craft knife, or a razor blade stuck into a cork. The design can be cut in negative or relief—i.e. either cut out the pattern you wish to make, or cut away the rubber leaving the pattern standing out. Either the edge-side of the rubber, or the flat surface, can be cut, first pencilling out the motif. If the flat surface is used, it is advisable, when it is cut, to glue it with impact adhesive to a small block of wood, such as a child's building block, so that sufficient pressure can be applied, and the block put down and picked up easily. Either water-based paints or printer's inks can be used—oil-based paints can be a bit sticky: the paint should be thick enough that it will adhere easily to the rubber block, but not so thick that the impression will be smudgy. Commercial inking pads, used for rubber stamping, are particularly good for these blocks.

LINO-CUTS

I will not go into this in great detail because, like wood-blocks, it is possible to get specialist books on the subject for delicate and intricate work. I myself make very rudimentary small lino-cuts, perhaps an inch (2.5 cm) square, cut into very simple forms such as a leaf, using lino-cutting tools. It is of course much easier with lino-cuts to get a more detailed block than with the other media we have discussed— potato, rubber, etc. I stick the small motif with impact adhesive on to a child's wooden building block, so that I have a handle with which to press the lino-cut firmly on the inking pad and then down on to the paper. Larger lino-cuts should be inked with a roller to get even coverage: the paint is mixed on the glass sheet, and evenly spread with the roller. Another effective paper can be made by applying gold metallic paint, diluted if necessary with turpentine, on to a small lino-cut motif, such as a fleur-de-lys, and printing it out on a sheet of Ingres paper.

ROLLERS

Apart from using the rollers to apply the paints or inks to the larger blocks, the rollers themselves can be used as tools. One method is to stick small shapes (diamonds, squares, circles) cut out in felt on to the surface of the roller, using cow gum so that the shapes can be removed. The roller is inked by rolling on the glass sheet or inking pad, and then rolled across the sheet of paper, on which the raised felt shapes then make the impressions. If a very accurate version of this is required, the easiest way of doing it is to mark out the actual size and circumference of the roller on graph paper, and work out where your felt shapes should go. Transfer these markings to the roller by cutting out the

shapes on the graph paper, glueing the paper lightly and temporarily to the roller, and tracing through the outline of the shapes with a pencil.

Another method is to cut the roller itself with a very sharp craft knife into lines (this is more difficult than it sounds, and virtually impossible with very hard rollers). Ink the roller and run it over the paper in an irregular fashion; then clean it off and, using another coloured ink, repeat the process.

orizomegami

This is the Japanese art of folding and pleating rice paper (also called Jap. tissue), and dipping the corners and edges of the folded paper into small bowls of vegetable dyes. The wet paper is then carefully unfolded to reveal the colours which the absorbent rice paper has picked up. The practice sounds deceptively simple, because in fact, by various means, very sophisticated papers looking like stained glass can be achieved by improving on this initial step.

Materials *Paints* These paints are traditionally vegetable dyes, of the consistency of ink. They can be bought from grocers or supermarkets, usually in the section for home baking, as these colours are mostly used for tinting icing sugars for cakes. Cochineal immediately springs to mind, but there are a surprising variety of colours—blue, green, yellow, violet—and since they are usually very cheap to buy, it is a good idea to have as wide a selection as possible.

Paper This has to be rice paper, since it is essential to have a soft, absorbent paper which will take up the colours easily. It is sold by the roll in art shops, and is not at all expensive.

Equipment Small bowls, such as cocotte dishes, or baked-bean tins, are used to contain the various dyes.
A pair of pliers, or tweezers, is very useful, though not essential.
You will also need clean uncrumpled newspaper.

Method Pour the various dyes into the containers, standing them on newspaper. Make sure you have a clean, completely flat surface on which to fold the rice paper. I find it useful to have a large pressing board, formica-faced, for this purpose. Then cut off some lengths of rice paper from the roll, and cut a pile of clean newspaper, larger by some inches all round than the pieces of rice paper. Have also to hand some small pieces of cardboard, or some small squares of newspaper (I find an old telephone directory very useful).

Now fold your rice paper: this must always be done in accordion pleats, so that each edge of the folded paper can absorb the dyes. First fold it along the length, or breadth, of the paper, so that you have neat,

even pleats. To achieve this, it is easiest to fold the paper in half, then fold each half towards the centre, and then open it up, and fold, in accordion fashion, towards the creases you have made. This is your initial folding. After this, the long pleats can be folded again into squares, rectangles, or triangles. Care must be taken that the paper is very neatly and evenly folded. Once this is done, and you have a small package of folded paper ready for dipping, I find it useful to hold it between a pair of pliers, or tweezers; this serves two purposes—first, the paper is firmly gripped in its pleats and folds; second, in dipping the paper into the pots you do not get vegetable dye on your fingers. Although the dyes are quite harmless, being edible, they are very strong, and it takes a lot of soaking and bleach to remove the stains from your hands and under your fingernails. (One can understand the success the ancient Britons had with woad.)

Holding the package of pleated paper firmly, dip each corner into a separate pot of dye. Then put the paper between bits of cardboard, or a small pile of newsprint, and press down firmly with your hand, so that the colours are evenly spread.

After this, most carefully unfold the paper on the large pile of cut newsprint. Great care must be taken to unfold it pleat by pleat, as the wet paper can easily tear. Remove the finished paper, keeping it on the sheet of newsprint for easy handling, and put it somewhere safe to dry (this does not take very long, half an hour or so).

Your initial efforts will be quite simple, with the colours spaced out separately and evenly. It is, however, worth practising in this way, to get the feel of the folding and pleating, and the method of dipping into the inks, colouring the edges as well as the corners, for example. Once this has been satisfactorily mastered, then more imaginative techniques can be used.

If the folded paper, held by the pliers or tweezers, is first quickly immersed in a small bowl of clear water before being dipped into the colours, you will find it has been made more receptive to the dyes, and the colours will flow into each other, instead of remaining separate—this is what creates the 'stained glass' effect.

Another technique is to put a single colour into two containers, and dilute one of them with water. The paper is then dipped first into the undiluted colour, then into the diluted, which creates a very pretty monochrome paper.

The paper can also be folded and dyed as usual, but with one or two corners or edges left untouched. Then, when the paper is dry, it can be refolded, and the previously untouched edges dipped in water, which causes the original colour to outline sharply the paler areas.

It is also possible, once one is a bit more skilled, to fold the paper diagonally, in a fan shape, and although this is rather more difficult, it creates a very interesting pattern.

When the paper is dry, it can be pressed between boards, or ironed carefully with a warm iron. The fold marks will remain, as they have been pressed in, but this is part of the tradition of orizomegami.

# craquelure/resist batik

The word craquelure is used to describe fine cracks in the paint or varnish on the surface of a picture. Batik is a Javanese word meaning 'drawing', and is a process of painting a pattern in wax on material, dyeing the part left exposed, and then removing the wax with heat. There were some very handsome papers made by this method in Germany in the twenties, but mechanical means were used to melt and control the wax at an even temperature and liquidity, and heated rollers used to apply it.

After a lot of trial and error I evolved three different methods of applying the wax without mechanical means, and although the re-sultant papers do not begin to compare with the richness and technique of, say, the German papers, they have a certain appeal, and are quite different from other decorative papers.

Materials	*Wax*	Candles, wax crayons, or a block of paraffin wax (from chemist or drug store), depending on your chosen method.
	Paints	Tubes of water-colour, poster paint, designer's gouache.
	Paper	Good quality typing, cartridge paper, Kraft (brown paper), sugar paper.
	Equipment	Plastic-coated garden wire of varying thickness, and pliers. Large (3″–4″, 7.5 cm–10 cm) paintbrush.

Method 1
Of the three methods I have experimented with, two use pre-heated wax, and the third cold.

For the first of the pre-heated methods I used candle-ends, and cheap wax crayons. Lay the paper to be decorated on a smooth pile of news-paper. Stand a lighted candle in an old saucer, and heat a candle-end or wax crayon in the flame until it drips. If the candle-end or crayon grows too hot to hold comfortably, it can be attached to a piece of wire bent into a holder. When the tip of the candle-end or crayon is

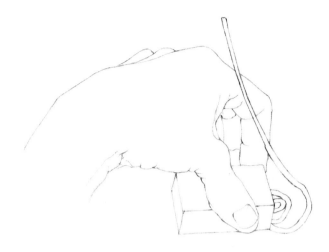

liquid, use it to draw designs on the paper. This is a fairly rudimentary process, as it is difficult to control the liquid wax: it often falls in heavy blobs, or hardens too quickly on contact with the paper, giving a very uneven effect. It is possible, when the wax is dry, to scrape off some of the heavier lumps with a kitchen knife.

Mix up your paint in a cereal bowl, or something similar, wide enough to take the large paintbrush easily. Then charge your brush with the paint, which should not be too thick, and colour-wash quickly and lightly all over the sheet, and put it somewhere flat, on newspaper, to dry out. When it is completely dry, iron it with a warm iron between sheets of newspaper, so that the wax dissolves into the newspaper.

Method 2 The second heated method is rather more controlled. For this you need a block of paraffin wax from a chemist, an old bowl in which to melt the wax, and a shape made by twisting one end of a 12″ (30 cm) length of plastic-coated wire, with pliers, into a simple shape; the other end is left upright to form a handle. Put the bowl containing the block of wax over a saucepan of water, and heat until the wax is completely liquid and translucent.

If possible, try to have your work area near the stove, as the wax hardens surprisingly quickly away from the heat, and is then impossible to use. As before, put the paper to be decorated on a pile of clean uncrumpled newspaper. Warm the wire shape for a minute or two in the hot wax before starting to use it, then shake off the excess wax and press the shape down firmly on to your paper to make a wax impression. You may find it useful to have a small block of wood, or a tin lid, with which to press the shape itself down on to the paper, as you cannot get much pressure from the wire handle. Quickly lift off the shape, re-dip in the hot wax, and continue with the impressions, remembering always to shake off the excess wax over the bowl in order to avoid blobs. When the wax is hard, colour-wash the paper as before with your large paintbrush, and, when it is completely dry, iron the paper between sheets of newspaper until the wax is melted and absorbed.

Method 3 Perhaps, strictly speaking, this third method should not come under the heading of 'resist', because the wax is not melted off, but simply softened. Since the crayons used are wax ones, however, it seems to fall more naturally into this section than any other, although the finished paper is different from the craquelure one.

I used some rather expensive Swiss oil crayons in various colours; unlike the previous methods where the wax is translucent, the colour of the crayons is visible, and forms part of the finished paper. I scribbled at random with one colour after another, all over a sheet of paper slightly thicker than usual (Kraft, thick cartridge, Ingres), and then ironed the sheet. The colours melted very slightly, and glazed the paper a little. I found this very effective on a dark red Ingres, which I had scribbled on diagonally with white, turquoise and dark blue crayons. It made an excellent, restrained modern paper, suitable for book-covers, etc. When I used a white cartridge, I gave it a colour wash, as in the first two methods, before ironing.

stencil papers

Stencils were widely used in Europe from the fifteenth century onwards as a means of colouring woodcuts, maps, etc., which by then were being printed; later, fashion plates were treated in this way. A different stencil was cut for each separate colour.

As a child I found stencilling very disappointing; my efforts ended up with blurred and smudgy outlines, very different from the crisp designs I had envisaged. It was not until comparatively recently, when I discovered the pleasures of stencilling with felt pens and felt markers, that I became more interested in the process, and started to investigate it.

Materials

Paints Acrylic paint, poster paint, printer's inks, felt pens (including gold and silver) and felt markers.

Paper Good quality typing paper, writing paper, cartridge and Ingres.

Thick cartridge or thin Manilla card for making stencils, and boiled linseed oil.

Equipment Commercial stencils if used.

Sharp craft knife, small nail scissors, ruler.

Stencil brushes of varying sizes, man-made sponges.

Small scrubbing-brush or nailbrush, nail-file or comb.

Method 1 There are many good, ready-made stencils of various sizes and designs available from art shops, and they usually come in a pack complete with detailed instructions for use. So in this section we will deal with stencils that you can make or adapt yourself, as this gives much more scope for individuality.

To make the stencil sheet, take some strong cartridge paper or thin Manilla card, and sponge it over well with boiled linseed oil. Hang it up to dry for about a day. When the oil dries, you will have a sheet of translucent stencil paper, ready for cutting. I find this much easier than the sheets of acetate sometimes recommended, as acetate seems rather difficult to cut, especially if one wants to make curved sections; whereas this paper, laid flat on a cutting board or mat, cuts very easily and smoothly with a sharp craft knife.

Work out on a separate sheet of paper the design you want to make, and, when you are happy with it, go over it with a dark felt pen. This pen can then be used to trace off your design on to the stencil sheet itself. At this stage, keep the design very simple, rather like a silhouette. If you want to make symmetrical designs, these can most easily be done by folding an ordinary sheet of paper in two, or four, or folded over into a triangular shape, and then cutting out sections from the folded edges (not the straight ones) with scissors—curved nail scissors are very useful. This, when unfolded, gives you an immediate, formal stencil pattern, ready to be traced off on to your stencil paper for cutting.

Place the prepared stencil paper on your sheet of paper, taping it if necessary to the surrounding area on which you are working. Felt

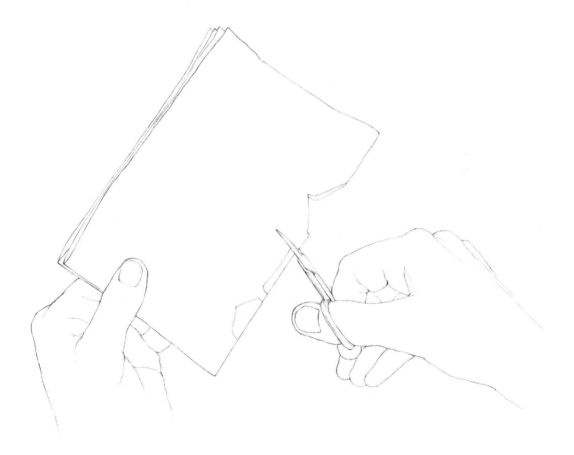

pens used for stencilling give a very sharp outline, as do markers (wide-tipped felt pens), which also cover the area to be stencilled very quickly and evenly. I also discovered by chance that a black marker I was using on Ingres paper transferred the pattern to both sides of the sheet, in a clean and inexplicable manner. This would be particularly effective for a frontispiece to a book, for example, where both sides could be seen. Acrylic paints can be used straight from the tube if a strong colour is wanted. Simply squeeze some of the paint on to a saucer, and apply the paint to the stencil with a small piece of man-made sponge, or a dry stencil brush. If you are using a brush, all excess paint should first be removed on a piece of newspaper, leaving the brush virtually dry, otherwise the paint will run under the stencil and give a blurred or

smudged outline. (This is why I like felt pens and markers so much, as with them there is no danger of that happening.) Hold your stencil brush upright, and dab it up and down: when you have finished, be careful not to slide the stencil as you lift it. Check that there is no paint on the underside before you proceed. With this form of decorated paper it is quite important to keep regular lines (unlike, say, block-printing, where a slight irregularity is acceptable), and it is sometimes advisable to rule light, pencil guidelines on the sheet to be stencilled.

If the area you want to cut out is a large one, or if you want to use more than one colour on, say, a flower, then you will have to break up your design, leaving a bridge of stencil paper to connect the cut-out areas. The best way of seeing how to do this in the least fussy manner is to look at commercial stencils.

Method 2   There is one other form of stencilling which should be referred to here, as it is certainly a form of decorated paper, although the finished form of this is very different, and much less formal. Various shapes—

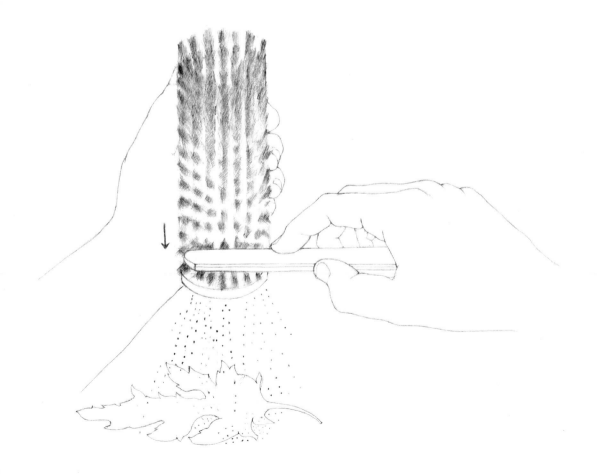

natural ones such as leaves, or others cut from thin cardboard—are arranged on the sheet to be stencilled, which should be lying on a large sheet of newspaper. (This is rather a messy process.) Mix up some water-based paint (poster, acrylic) in a bowl wide enough to take a stiff-bristled brush (small scrubbing-brush or nailbrush). Charge the brush with colour, but knock off the excess on a pad of newspaper. Then holding the brush in one hand, bristles upwards, draw a piece of stiff card or a nail-file across it, causing a spray of paint to be thrown down on to the sheet. (Note: draw the card or nail-file towards you, so that the spray of colour falls away from you on to the sheet.) It is possible to vary the intensity of the paint spray by holding the brush closer to or farther from the paper. When the paper has been stippled, remove the shape, exposing the area which has been protected from the spray. Although initial efforts may appear rather coarse, it is possible to get fine effects by using interesting monochrome in, say, Venetian red, or else using two nailbrushes and two separate stippling colours.

oil marbling

In oil marbling, the colours are not applied directly to the paper, but floated on the surface of a tray, or bath, of liquid. The patterns that form are then transferred to a sheet of paper laid down on the surface of the bath. This is quite simple, and can be mastered in a few hours; it is a very immediate and satisfying way of decorating paper.

Materials   *Paints*   Tubes of students' oil paints are best: the more expensive paints are more difficult to mix.
Turpentine for diluting the colours.

Paper   Good quality typing paper, cartridge, and for special papers, Ingres.

Base liquid   Cellulose wallpaper paste (Method 1); cold-water wallpaper paste (method 2).

Equipment   Small cheap brushes for mixing up the colours.
Glass or plastic eye-droppers or pipettes for dropping the colours on the surface.
Plastic seed box or cat-litter tray to contain the liquid approximately 12″ × 15″ (30 cm–37 cm).
Small pots to contain the oil paints (old cups, or small baked-bean tins).
Wood stylus or pencil, coarse plastic comb.
Newspaper.
Large plastic ice-cream container or equivalent.

Method 1   Mix up the liquid for the bath an hour or so in advance in a plastic bucket, following the manufacturer's directions but adding considerably more water than is recommended. You do not want a paste, you are simply thickening the water to a consistency of thin cream to make it more manageable. If it is too thick, add more water, stirring vigorously so that there are no lumps.

Cover your work surface with newspaper, as you are using oil paints which are not water-soluble, and so can make rather a mess.

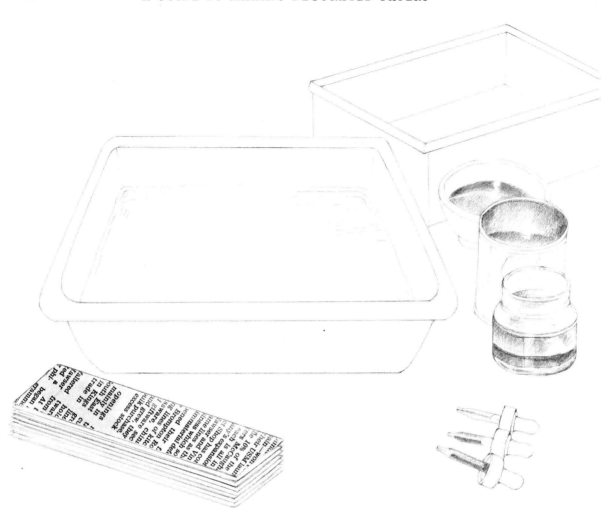

Squeeze out about ½″ (1 cm) black oil paint into one of your pots, add a little turpentine, and mix well until the paint is dissolved. Add more turpentine drop by drop until the paint is quite diluted, and can be easily taken up by the eye-dropper or pipette. Mix up two more colours in the same way. Cut a pile of newspaper to the size of your bath—this is used for taking up any paint left on the surface of the bath between marbling the sheets of paper, and cut a pile of strips of paper, about 2″ (5 cm) in depth, the size of the width of your bath, which will be used for skimming the surface. You will also need something like a large plastic ice-cream container to hold the used and dirty newspaper.

When you are ready, pour some of the base liquid (the thin cellulose paste) into the tray, to a minimum depth of 3″ (7.5 cm). Fill your droppers with paint, and line up the pots by the side of the bath, ready to hand. Quickly skim the surface of the bath from front to back with your newspaper skimming strip, and drop spots of your first colour, which is usually black, on to the surface of the bath. These drops should spread evenly and quickly into circles of about 2″–3″ (5 cm–6 cm) in diameter. If the colour does not spread, but sinks to the bottom of the bath, add more turpentine, mix well, and try again. Add the turpentine drop by drop, testing all the time on the surface of the bath, because if the paint is too diluted it is very difficult to use. Continue until the black spreads as you want it to, cleaning off the bath in between tries with a piece of cut newspaper laid flat on the surface to take up the paint. When you are successful with the black, try out your next colour, by dropping it as nearly as possible into the

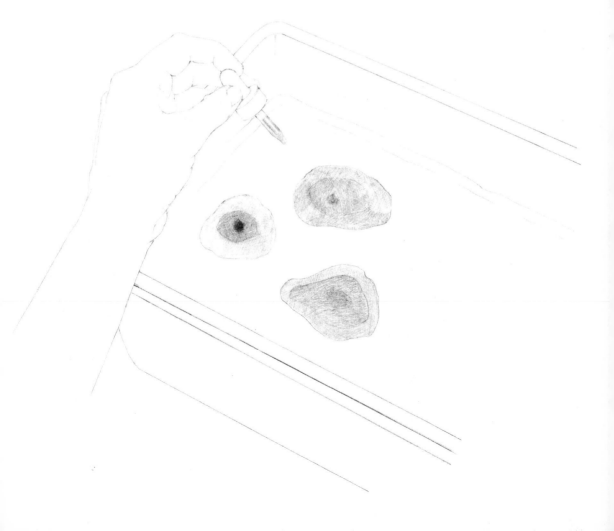

centre of the black circles. If you are fortunate, this next colour will expand in the same way, leaving a wide black rim (your first colour) round the edge of the circle. If this colour does not spread satisfactorily, continue to add turpentine as before, mixing well. When you are successful, drop your third colour into the centre of the circles, so that you now have two wide rims round your third colour.

Transfer these colours to the paper by gently laying the sheet **on the** surface of the bath. The best way to do this is to hold the right-hand bottom corner in your right hand, and the top left corner in your left hand, and starting with the right hand, lay the paper slowly down in a diagonal fashion, making sure no bubbles of air are trapped beneath the paper. Then pull the paper towards you, holding the two bottom corners, dragging it slightly over the edge of the bath so that surplus moisture is drained off. Put the sheet down flat, face up, on your newspaper to dry, and clean the bath by laying a cut sheet of newspaper on the surface to pick up any paint which has been left behind.

Once you have mastered this basic technique, you can start to experiment with your patterns. You can draw a stylus (wooden pencil) through the circles, and the paints will form interesting but always separate lines and swirls. You can also comb the colours by using a coarse plastic comb with alternate teeth removed with pliers. For combing, you may find it easier to use a slightly thicker bath, as with a very thin bath the surface sometimes does not hold the patterns satisfactorily. Always remember to clean the bath between each marbling by laying down newspaper on the surface, and also always remember to skim the surface of the bath before dropping on your paint, so that there is no surface tension to prevent the paint from spreading.

It is possible to keep and use the bath for several days, but you may also find that, even in one day, the bath quite suddenly becomes saturated with paint, and your papers no longer look fresh and clean. When that happens, throw away the liquid and start again.

Method 2   There is another, completely different way of oil marbling, invented and perfected by Marie-Ange Doizy, a French marbler and lecturer. Instead of a thin cellulose base, Marie-Ange uses an extremely thick one—almost, but not quite, solid. A cold-water wallpaper paste (not cellulose, which is too grainy) can be used, stirred into a small amount of water, to create a blancmange type of base. Using a flat brush of perhaps 1½″ (4 cm) width, the oil paint, thinned as before with turpentine, is brushed on to the almost solid surface of the bath in a wide band of colour. Subsequent colours are similarly brushed on in adjoining stripes, and the pattern is then combed through with a coarse comb; it can be cross-combed, and counter-combed. Note that the brushes will inevitably pick up some paste as you brush them across the bath, and this should be scraped off before replacing the brushes in their respective paint pots. When the combing is complete, the paper is laid down on the bath, as before, on the finished pattern, and drawn off.

Very clear and interesting effects can be achieved by this method, first described in a book called *Le Papier Marbré*, which Marie-Ange Doizy wrote with Stephan Ipert.

suminagashi

The Japanese have a very beautiful and old form of art, called sumi-nagashi, where inks are floated on a tray of clear water, and then gently blown on, or manipulated with a thin stick, so that the inks form delicate patterns. The true art takes many years to learn (like Japanese flower arrangement), but it is possible to do it in a simplified form, and I was amazed and delighted when I first tried it. To start with, it is simplicity itself to set up, and the work of a moment to clear it away when you have finished. It can provide instant entertainment for a child, and is not at all a messy process, unlike oil marbling. The effects are very pretty and delicate, and if one is using a small bath, or tray, writing paper can be marbled, and then used as a very individual kind of stationery, as it is quite possible to write legibly on the finished paper.

Materials   *Inks*   Indian ink or Chinese ink (also called drawing inks).
                  Paper   Any good quality paper.
                  Equipment   A tray (baking tray, ceramic dish), of some two or three inches (4 cm–6 cm) in depth, and large enough to accommodate your sheet of paper.
                                  Several small slender sticks (such as orange sticks, sharpened matchsticks, nails or pencils).

Method   Fill the tray with clear water. Dip the stick or nail into the bottle of ink most carefully, then touch the tip on the surface of the water, allowing one drop only of the ink to fall into the centre of the tray. It will quickly spread. Then take another little stick, and either pass it through your hair (to collect a minute amount of grease), or put a little oil or grease on your hand, and touch the point of the stick to it. The result is to make the tip lightly greased, to make it water-resistant. Then swirl the point of the stick through the ink, to create marbled patterns. Pick up your sheet of paper, rest it gently on the surface, then carefully lift it off. The 'marbled' effect will have transferred itself to your paper, which you should then leave somewhere flat, face up, to dry completely, before pressing it.

Two, three, or four colours of ink can be used, one lightly dropped on top of the other, and then swirled. The only thing that has to be learnt, if the effects are to be elegant, is just to touch the surface of the

water with the tiniest amount of ink on the tip of the nail or stick. If the drop is too big, it will be too heavy to rest on the surface of the water, and will sink.

When the water in the dish becomes dirty, simply tip it out and start again. Sometimes, however, if one is using more than one colour, little specks get left behind on the surface; these can form a pretty background for the next sheet you marble.